Unfathc

Phantasmagoria

Jahméne

ISBN: 9781521439135

Unfathomable Phantasmagoria

The trail of dreams that move through space and time like a whisper of memories shadowing you to your present day, passing you into your future. Ever close in time but not yet completely fathomed, not yet fully explored or understood. A dream infinite in possibilities beyond our own understanding; we don't know the depth but we venture forward into its wonder regardless.

A collection of poems written by Jahméne.

CONTENTS

1	Side Of Love	Pg 1-2
2	Shadow Serpent	Pg 3-4
3	Time	Pg 5-6
4	Eyes	Pg 7
5	A Strong Faith Is Contagious	Pg 8
6	Freedom	Pg 9
7	Against The Odds	Pg 10
8	Stars	Pg 11
9	The Way	Pg 12
10	Seasons Of Love	Pg 13
11	Marinading Moments	Pg 14-15
12	Daring	Pg 16
13	Blush: A Dream	Pg 17
14	Secrets	Pg 18
15	Take Me	Pg 19
16	Not Knowing	Pg 20-21
17	Complete & Whole	Pg 22-23
18	Devoured	Pg 24-26
19	Searching For Love	Pg 27-28
20	The Things We Do For Love	Pg 29
21	My Eyes Reflect The Water	Pg 30-31
22	Stolen Seconds	Pg 32-33

23	Dancing Spirit; Life Of Fire. (A Message For Mother.)	Pg 34-35
24	Hustle Bustle	Pg 36-37
25	Keeping Magic	Pg 38
26	Us	Pg 39
27	Illuminated Darkness	Pg 40
28	Fear The Fire In His Eyes	Pg 41-42
29	Brought To Blindness	Pg 43
30	Don't Give Up	Pg 44
31	Blessed Rain	Pg 45-47
32	Remember	Pg 48
33	Strawberries & Cream	Pg 49-50
34	Imagine Intimacy	Pg 51-52
35	Tension	Pg 53-55
36	Learning Lasting Love	Pg 56-57
37	Tired Of Lonely?	Pg 58-59
38	Heart Guardian: The Love Behind Brown Eyes.	Pg 60-61
39	Trust In Time	Pg 62-63
40	Eternity & Forever	Pg 64-65
41	Deadly Waters	Pg 66-67
42	I Am	Pg 68
43	She Flies: The Phoenix	Pg 69-70

44	A Message For A Friend	Pg 71
45	Fruitless Father	Pg 72-73
46	Brief Moments	Pg 74-75
47	Take Me There	Pg 76-77
48	Your Voice	Pg 78-79
49	Prance Around The Serious	Pg 80-81
50	Muddied Waters	Pg 82-84
51	Love	Pg 85-86
52	I Need You Now	Pg 87
53	Dear God	Pg 88
54	Zzz ...	Pg 89-90
55	Break Open	Pg 91
56	The Thickness Of Our Bark	Pg 92-93
57	Destructive Tears	Pg 94-95
58	Deceiver	Pg 96
59	Suicidal Possession	Pg 97-100
60	Droplets Of Change	Pg 101
61	Weakening Anger	Pg 102
62	Count Your Blessings	Pg 103
63	Dig A Little Deeper	Pg 104
64	Identities Lost	Pg 105-107
65	Dreamers	Pg 108
66	Morning Story	Pg 109

67	Suppression	Pg 110
68	Roses	Pg 111
69	Pretty Path	Pg 112
70	Intentional Mistakes	Pg 113
71	Just Ask	Pg 114
72	A Memories Ghost	Pg 115-116
73	Salvation	Pg 117
74	Thorny Temptation	Pg 118 -119
75	Finding Freedom Forgiving Father	Pg 120-122

I would like to dedicate this book to my beautiful mother.

An inspiration in every way; from being a creative free spirit, to teaching me how to walk and talk right. Thank you for being someone who has always loved me unconditionally. Your heart is so pure and I'm eternally grateful for your strength, wisdom, passion and love. You never cease to amaze me with your creativity and spirit.

Love You Always,
- Your Son.

Side of Love

My slanted brows
my squinted eyes
the cool minds whisper
came as no surprise.
My face is sullen
my mouth is still
Dare move my stare?
My voice might spill.

My hands entwined
my legs are steady
my hips may twitch
just before I'm ready.
My lungs are tired
my heart is racing
a stance of strength
towards those I'm facing.

You can't shift the man
who refuses to move
In a place that he believes in.
You can strip me down
to the very bone;
still my faith won't wear thin.

You can tire me of my human flesh
and take my riches for plunder
but my spirit lies in a deeper place
that no man can put asunder.

You can preach your words of lies
you can spit your horrid ways
you may mock and insult me

but still, this heart you can't erase.

My arms are heavy
my lids are closing
days may drip on into weeks
but still you are not imposing.

For the side of love
is a wall of height
which you can never climb.
You may snarl and you may bite
but it will stand the test of time.

The difference between you and I
is that hate drives itself out.
Love is an over powering thing
one thing I will never doubt.

So as you rest your head to sleep
exhausted from your attempted slaying
I'll be there by your side
hand in hand
kneeling
and
forever praying.

Shadow Serpent

Serpent of the shadows
deliverer of the dark
slithering through vision
without leaving a mark.

Snaked into the corner
of the blindness of my eye
trick to flick the other way
where your presence does not lie.

Burnt out spots of death
my soul you must retrieve
your breath stains the air
I know you want me to believe.

To trip into your dungeon
where the drips pass away the time
break me down thought by thought
until my mind's no longer mine.

Like clay you want to mould me
into something to control
cowering and shivering
no longer feeling whole.

But in my very last exhale
will be the moment you freeze in place
as the life leaves my mouth
and burns your hidden face.

Your tears fall back down to me
as my eyes begin to fall
sinking to a realisation

that you never had me at all.

For that tireless wicked torment
you desired to put me through
forgot one thing about me
but I know all about you.

My heart holds something powerful
a spirit that repulses evils name
you flee back to where you crept from
and His love and life I shall regain.

I do not believe the whipping words
that slash across my back
I just know your horrid actions
are because of all the things **you** lack.
So continue to bite the layers
you **think** may weaken my faith
but i'll remind you when it's not working
that I'm from a much different place.

A place where I was taught
that darkness can't burn out the light
but light will **always** guide me through
the deadly dying demons of the night.

Your weight upon my chest
does not crush my pounding heart
but a single word of gospel truth
will tear
your world
apart.

Time

A simple smile
A loving kiss
A number you dial
A call that you miss.

The hand of the second
the eyes on the hour
time is pushing your life
as you watch it devour
the minutes you had
the people you know
all forced into memories
as you watch yourself grow.

As the journey continues
who is left by your side?
Did you take them for granted
along your vicious ride?
Did you think that it mattered
what each second cost
in disagreements and anger
how much time you had lost?

Is it time that you realised
how precious it is?
Has it struck your mind
just how precious it is ?

That smile that you shared
Those lips that you kissed
That number you dialled
Or the one that you missed.

A person in your life
will not always be there
A life is a life
show that you care.

Can you not see
it's almost hit twelve.
What will you do
when death comes to delve?
It will suddenly knock
and open your eyes
the time you've wasted
on hatred and lies.

You will wish you could do
what no one can do
winding it back
past the nine and the two.

Make a change now
make it today
appreciate life
in e v e r y way.

Eyes

What's the story behind your eyes?
Crinkled laughter? A dark surprise?
Open truth or shut closed lies?
What's the story behind those eyes?

A Strong Faith Is Contagious

A reflection of yourself
empathetic waves
collapsing foundations
dangerous caves.

Don't shout too loud
don't move too fast
you'll break the silence
and shake the past.

For what you've done to others
may paint the walls with acid
if the intentions were not pure
and reactions were not placid.

You can fill in the appearing cracks
but can't shift the rubble alone.
Go back before the damage is final
and make your heart a home.

Housing love and wisdom,
growth and finding nothing but happy things
So when your mind is opened
A contagious faith will soar with valiant wings.

Freedom

How free is freedom
inside the box of a closed mind?
Ignorance makes the unique
curl up and hide.
Freedom is where you find it
Open up your mind.

Against The Odds

When my voice was stolen
dreams were taken
and every answer was no.
I looked in deeper places
friendly faces
to ignite my light to grow.

Stars

Looking up at the stars at night
I feel like we are so small
but there's one thing much bigger
our love that sits on top of it all.

The Way

Moonlight, stars and pitch black sky
explain to me the reasons why
even though you reside so high
I still feel the tears you cry.

Moonlight, stars and pitch black sky
life's not over when you die
inside is where the power lies
just spread your wings to fly.

Twinkle bright
guide the night
take on height
upon the flight.

Moonlight, stars and pitch black sky
I'll say I love you
before goodbye
and from minds pocket
you will pry
the truth from eye to eye.

Moonlight, stars
A brand new day
listen to what wisdom says
and then you can only pray
that you've found the way.

Seasons of Love

Mind deep decays as the shallow case of my comfort is taken
with a stranger.
Flicked into the spaces dancing through summer, autumn,
winter and spring.
My attention held captive by the unknown force that drives the
movement
the pounding of my feet matching the lonely song that I sing.

Taken with a stranger with eyes slant and intriguing.
Taken with a possible danger that could hurt without you
seeing.

Truthful is the feeling, but will a feeling last?
The seasons are all waiting to see if you pass.
The snow crunches darkness as you tighten in the cold
the leaves drop down in sepia as their smile lights up like gold
the warmth of refreshment when your hand they hold
the heat increases the pressure, yet still such beauty to behold.

Taken with a fantasy
A dream that could drift on by.
peeling back the layers
Asking yourself why ?
Flowing with the feeling
but will the feeling last?
hopeful is my intention
so set me to the task.

Marinading Moments

You crashed in on a space so deeply delicate
embracing my appreciation with signs so solid.
Stroking up on secretive and sensitive places
cracking open what I thought was so well hid.

Touching down on this plane of a new thing
pressing closely with a mist of enchantment.
Cornering my quietness until I'm forced to sing
pulling like a crazed puppeteer with such control.

A feeling bizarre
yet oddly pleasing.
Will it scar
or are you teasing?

This prominent heartbeat
Under toned pressure.
What is this rare treat?
A sweeping love refresher?

Lightly tickling the emotions on this thin skinned fantasy
knocking on the doors that are locked forever more.
Diving into pits of unimaginable dangerous depth.
I'm falling, falling
fast into your core.

Are you letting me in
or am I taking a peak?
Will your footsteps be heavy
or am I watching you creep?

Did you give me the key
to this forbidden lock?
Even if I got what I wanted
I'd still be in shock.

Dragging behind
so slowly in awe
will I make it in time
to be welcomed for more?
Will I?
Won't I?
Let us explore
The fountains of minutes
that trickle and pour
I'll collect them in buckets
So that we have time
Marinading in moments
until you are mine.

Daring

Intimate passion
future depression
infatuated sickness
character suppression.
Forced decisions
Murder witness
Virgin to your touch
Will it be too much?
Testing reactions dangers
Harbouring sensations
exploring dimensions.
A daring judge.

Blush: A Dream

Eyes of mystery
learning history
hesitating temptation.
Alluring words
Have you heard?
Attracting sensation.
Sipping fountains
love filled wells
dipping heart in heart.
Breaking tension
future mansion
realities future starts.

Secrets

Tell me your secrets
and i'll keep them
hidden in the deepest part of me.
If you tell me secrets
tear down that defence
and I promise to love you
unconditionally.

Take Me

Grab my hand and take me
steal my heart but don't break me
give me life and shake me
into a brand new walk with you.

Not Knowing

Youthful spirit
childish games
building trickery
pull in your reigns.
Misleading direction
foolish plans
demanding attention
frantic hands.
Shifting eyes
alluring attraction
wants and needs
desired reaction.
Touching feelings
grasping hearts
melting minds
all of the parts.
Taken for granted
shoved aside
hurtful actions
broken inside.
Treasured moments
chosen times
pick or drop me
the choice not mine.
Patiently waiting
scared for the call
either you will hold me
or push me to fall.
I beg you to be gentle
my world revolves you
if you were to hurt me
I dread what I'd do.

Trusting blindness
reaching out
guide me through
loudly shout.
Scream the truth
rattle the winds
let me hear
let it ring.
Balance my ego
tell me now
love me properly
show me how.
Take me entirely
or nothing at all
don't selfishly wound me
and leave me to crawl.
Hold my hand
whisper words
trickling emotions
let them be heard.

Complete & Whole

You crept softly with a walk so damaging.
Imprinted your way through to where I lay
I gradually evaporate with your entrance
Scared that you're here to watch me decay.

Build me up to be something more than I can dream.
Tear me down past the level of losing all control.

Imploding on the very thought of these outcomes
Exploding on the gathered emotions of daring
Dicing with what could be yours if you tried
Attempting to uncover all through simply sharing.

Feelings galore
a hearts tour
giving yourself
they still want more.

Tread carefully
love's paper thin
gambling drama
caving in.

Riddles through answers
questions unresolved
each retraction
a heart dissolved.

Embrace the growth that you have carefully made
entwined our core roots until you could no longer fade.
Stealing the fruits and now you're running afraid
leaving me empty when you should have stayed.

Lost in reaching
dropped the teaching
a distant preaching
from cupids screeching.
Chimed on the bells
in my future plan
your voice is ringing
ever since this began.
Now the fruits are stolen
i've lost all control
why won't you take me
complete and whole?

Devoured

Blood stained feathers fall.
Heartless skeletons wrapped around life
lacking remorse as they come to maul
picking apart the frail frame of standing weakness.

Unsympathetic are the eyes that may know you
just ruthless savages who wish to ravage and prey
as your sensitive soul shivers in sullenness
pecking at your balance until you falter and sway
sipping your essence away.

Your feet seem stuck although they are not bound by chains
your compassion for these shallow minds enslaves you.
Choking on the food you loyally gave in the size of grains
they're unable to digest that they do not understand
down passages so incoherent and plain.
Yet you still try and stay to explain
but what will remain of your patience
when the spirit bandits continue to complain.

They're not here to learn from your rich affectionate friendship.
They're here to steal from you bit by bit
as their claws chip
and their mouths drip.
They'll scrape the skull bare of your passionate benevolence
watching you drain yourself dry
until all character is left raw to strip
edging you to trip
because when your down or on your knees at least
they all swoop down to begin the feast.

Blood stained feathers fall,
but the blood's not theirs at all.
Vultures after your soul.
Muffled moans
empty cages.
Skin pulled tight around bones
as their crooked wings twitch
verging on unprovoked rages.

Feeding from your love
they gain nothing
and the faults not yours at all.

In that last plea for compassion
that last out stretched bough of hope
In all their cannibalistic fashion
They'll snatch out your eyes
and watch you slowly slope
back into the illusion they pulled over your intelligence
as their talons scatter to grope.

They swirled around your understandings until it made you
irritably distracted
overwhelmed you with testing your persistent perseverance as
you perched.
Attracted to the challenge, oblivious, as your energy was
extracted.
You attempt to leave but the deception is too deep.
Now what's left of the power you keep?

Blood stained feathers fall,
but the blood is not theirs at all.
I'm sure there's not one moment you can recall
that they've stopped to let you thrive in your being
and there's no guaranteeing
that they'll even stop
when you're battered into your crawl.

No need to stay and question motives.
No need to stay to watch those last feathers fall.
These are vultures at their finest
they won't retire until they've devoured you all.

1 Peter 5:8
'Be sober, be vigilant; because your adversary the devil, as a roaring lion, walketh
about, seeking whom he may devour.'

Searching For Love

The sweet hesitant echoed keys of a piano disseminating mixed feelings of desperation, emptiness and hope in the distant background.
The swift breeze passes through the still ambiance sneaking softly past you, gently embracing your face, alluring you into a state of serenity.
Silent whispers through serene surroundings, causing the cessation of focus to the now faded setting. There are words to the one, taken from a hole in you so deep ...

But where are you?

Smoothed over the corners of reality to suit your needs.
A forced mist of a dream planted over the eyes
bring forth the plans of the dream into light
and make it now.

But where are you?

A hallucination, delusion, dream, spectre?
Here in your absoluteness?
On your way?

Movements are slow for time has no meaning here in this space
I reside mentally. Sliding my hands past the over grown open land with a feeling of depletion, emptiness, a longing to be cherished.

Facing forward
looking behind.

Eyes blinded by the sun; a vision impaired by what I want to see but my heart shelters me from.

Where are you?

I am instantly drawn to your reply which is now vividly painted in my mind and it vibrates through my whole being.
It's even closer than the tranquility of my judicious thoughts, my assumptions of what is to be ...

'Stop searching for love. You have forgotten me because you've experienced so much anguish in the past. I am right here. I have been here all along and I will always be ... Love.'

The Things We Do For Love

Unintentional damage through hearts confusion
floating broken until we reach the conclusion.
Lost in a pain so devouring and deep
unexplainable risky reasons behind the leap.
You just did and you've done
hoping you would've won,
but instead they've left you to fall from above.
Why do we foolishly entrust others with ourselves ?

We simply do it all for love.

My Eyes Reflect The Water

My eyes reflect the water
my lips bounce back the words
flowing down my river
with sounds that go unheard.
My depth speaks in volumes
yet my movement passes you by
unnoticed I remain
as I collect the tears you cry.

My strength may not be visible
it may seem I've grown worn and weak
but I'm picking up my speed
still moving, whether shallow or deep.

I grind with rocks to carve my pathway
I push the stones against the tide
I'll find my place through obstacles
until I've spread out far and wide.

I can settle in the summer
with the warmth of my heart pouring out
but by winters arrival
your actions to dive in i'll always doubt.
Afraid to take that leap
into the darkness of my season
just taking what you want from me
avoiding all bonding adhesion.

I don't blame you for being shallow
to get to know my mind so deep
but draining me of my waters
leaves me with eyes that no longer weep.

Because my eyes reflect the water
this coursing journey that I'm on
i'm focused on my future
I know where i'm coming from.
You can drink from the valleys
you can sip from my mind
i'll keep on moving
leaving your rocks behind.

I refuse to carry weighty obstacles
but you can live inside my being
don't expect me to pay attention
and I won't always be agreeing.

I am moving like a river
I can settle like the sea
I can drop like a waterfall
and i'll always be free.

Take from me what you will
whether for greed or personal gain
just remember I have a quantity
and I won't always remain.
Don't expect me to be tolerant
don't be surprised when I escape
you'll miss me when I'm gone
and you'll follow my pathways scrape.
When you have caught up with me
I can only hope that you would have learned
I can love you when you're hating
but i'll be gone until you've returned
with the knowledge of fully knowing
that my ever flowing love
Is something that must be earned.

Stolen Seconds

Captivating were those eyes of yours
tore through my barrier of self control
oddly moving were the words you chose
Insignificant
but my heart held onto every word.

Brief are these memorable moments
that I may never get to witness again
but for now i'll not wipe them away
like light rain on my window pane.

Finding myself lost in a moment …

Between the bustling duration of us passing
and the direction of your vision
like the halving of night and day
our worlds have a division.

How embarrassed I would be
if you were to call me out on it.
For you it would be so easy
yet i'd be relieved that you knew
or … would I be?

Mesmerising are those eyes of yours
where am I in my state of thought?
When my stare has passed the seconds
it's not on the ground I firmly stand
but somewhere far, one reckons.

Racing to the rhythm of this enchantment.
An idiosyncratic beat my heart does pound
as cupid flings back his arrow upon the bow
an intruding fear sweeps in

as my courage takes to the ground.

But calming are those eyes of yours
those eyes of silk
how love does pour
so flowingly
those eyes
those eyes
I cannot know
you blink
I stutter
and it hits me more.
Will I ever get to fathom?
Will I ever get to explore?
Will you let me hold that feeling?
Can we open up that door?

The life that has grasped me
through eyes I've grown to adore
that energy is so pulsating
i'm tongue tied
melting on the floor.

And ultimately,
as the clock hands
evaporate away the time,
will I get to know those eyes
your eyes
staring back at mine.

Dancing Spirit; Life of Fire

…A message for Mother…

Dancing spirit, life of fire
As the pressure increases
what will transpire?
Like the seed of a dandelion
floating higher and higher
where will you land
when you begin to tire?
Questions upon questions
getting to what you desire.
When do I get to peace
and who is the supplier?

Delving deeper into the space
through the dark along the wire
you'll travel further than others with your
dancing spirit and life of fire.

You are the piece you thought you had lost
it's your voice inside you need to accost
that voice that's pulled you through so far
was it beaten down with experiences scar?
Without the guidance from confidence in who you are
did you stray to a place with no leading star?
Looking up and around for something to fit the mould
a temporary fix which has you controlled.
Moving deeper and deeper into the land of the lost
It's your voice inside you need to accost.
It's your mind that needs to be told
to open the box of hidden treasures
that your heart so secretly holds.

Dancing spirit
life of fire
mind of doubt
heart entire.
Eyes of drama
lifes attire
learning to wear struggle
with the more you acquire.

Alive is your dancing spirit
let the rhythm take you away
dance until the trouble's away.
The flames are flickering
amongst your shuffling feet
with your life of fire
withstand the heat.

Only you know
what makes you complete.
When the drum stops
don't panic and run
pause and stay
until you feel you have won.
A history of pain
unravel all that was spun
it's your time now
So burn bright like the sun.

Hustle Bustle

Hustle bustle
your feet move faster than time
eyes are twitching
where's the placement of your mind?
Step on step
rushing through your history
not living your moments
or gaining any glory.
Hustle bustle
your feet move faster than time
huff and puff
when you've crossed so many lines.
You don't know where you're going
but you're travelling with speed
pace yourself for a second
before you take the lead.
Life is a blessing
the smallest measurement of it counts
so don't rush through your moments
with your rush rush
push push
squeezing ice into water
not realising the crush crush.
Living is a process
so just take your time
make sure you have control
of that all important mind.
Step from the street pavement
into your pathway of choice
don't be coaxed into direction
have an independent voice.
So when you stop for a minute
to say your fractioned part
you can stand tall and speak

all the words of your heart.
Not the silly little distractions
not the movement of the herd
not the things forced fed
but the truth and the word.
The love and light
that should easily be freed
not always the "norm"
or the agreed.
Take control of your mind
and the life that you lead.

Keeping Magic

Keep the magic of your dreams
in your every day thoughts.
Imaginations dream
always reaching for more
reality leans upon a liquid core;
life's balance of wants and needs.
Dream past the touchable
succeed past the dream
make it all watchable
as you float back down
memory stream.

Us

I just want it to be
you and me
free in the world
our future we see.
Fighting together in trials
but you just fight me.

Illuminated Darkness

The accumulation of a darkened obscuration eclipses your
illumination.
A hovering sensation amplifies itself within an abysmal inner
cavern.
Dominating what was aglow and superseding what you knew to
be legit,
devouring bit by bit a core so enduring and dense with life
experience.

Will you make it through the expedition past the evening tides
duskiness?
Forcibly hauled into its contagiously pessimistic depth with
putrid walls.
Can you disburden such a cancer that has plagued your
exuberance?

This delirium is your own undesirable creation
all within the asylum of a contorted mind.

Will the brilliance of a flame burn out the nightfall?
Calculating an entities existence;
time is revealing.

Set my being alight and see what joys shall come
keep the fire burning bright until the fight is won.

Fear The Fire In His Eyes

Stick my fingers in my ears
so I can not hear
afraid that if I do
I won't know that mommies here.
All I hear is screaming
but at least I know she's breathing
it's much too real to be dreaming
overwhelmed and drugged with fear.

Footsteps on the stairs
I know exactly who is there
a shadow haunting the dark
as he mumbles and he swears.
Silence fills this space
blurry eyes from crying
daddies got fire in his eyes.
Is my mommy dying?

I can hear each punch
groans of a woman in pain
forcing my head into my pillow
I can't take this all again.

I don't know if we'll see the daylight
she's crying out for some one to save her
accepting death on this night
perhaps then we will be free.

I was once controlled by fear
and I let it define who I was
poisoned by a demon
ignoring the root cause
hidden behind closed doors.

I was once controlled by fear
but I had to let go and move on
today i'm still standing strong
still breathing and still here.

Brought To Blindness

Tears fall from a thought
believing a foolish promise.
Safe from wild hands?
Plucked from danger?
Dropped into being caught
reigned in by blindness
drowned and muffled love
a confusing kindness.
Why did you bring me here?

Scars under the skin
hiding honesty scared
pretending wears thin.
Truth wets the tongue
burns lies into the mind
the road back is long.
Why did you bring me here?

Sorrow hits the ground
what I thought I knew is lost
in spaces never found.
The only way back in
is having you around.

Vision seems to disappear
dissolving riddled illusions
reality and truth
dirty windows
but I'm getting near.
Still one question remains unclear
Why did you pick me up
bring me to blindness
and drop me here?

Don't Give Up

Could you be the light to guide me to where I need to go?
Is this real that I can feel this way before the fight is won?
Gotta get down
before it's too late
the line of fire
the deadly hate.
Could it be that time to rise up?
Or could it be that time to simply stop?
Tell me again
don't give up.
I need to hear it
Don't give up!

Blessed Rain

I gave you all the diamonds from my soul
and now that sparkling feeling is gone
I don't know if i'm whole.

Stuck here like a fossil in a stone
blasting through an age of sadness
hear my hearts cry moan.

Therapy won't heal my troubles
because my pain runs deep
thick behind walls of no extraction
that's where my demons creep.

Waiting for harmonious bars to save me
where all uplifting notes shall meet
drained of all my energies
left on my knees and not my feet.

This desert I am traveling in
has sucked the moisture from my skin
my abyss has frozen over
but the ice is dangerously thin.

Look up to clouds of gentle pleasures
lost in what could have been mine
tired and exhausted
where are the joys in endless time?

Head boiled over
lucky clover
screams behind closed doors.
Fires are burning
stomaches churning
he's back to take some more.

Can you see the devil hid
set in eyes that gave me food
don't break this painful silence
I'll be killed from his angry mood.

Not a midnight darkness
not a moving shadow
awaken to my reality.
This shifting sadness
a broken madness
the devils creativity.

Bleeding hands where I held the rope
to salvage what I had.
Watched it floating
forever floating
until it smashed
and made him glad.

The presence may not be near
but still close is that stench of fear
buried way down inside cavernous memories
I know that it's forever here.

Front a smile
only for a while
but when the night will come
my mind will play its trickery
as my past will have its fun.

Please take me now
before I take myself
I only care for happiness
not unnecessary wealth.
Take me in arms of comfort
to make it all just fade away
save me from unwanted intentions
This is my cry for help.

Keep on moving
forever moving
To escape this pent up pain.
Waiting, waiting
forever waiting
for that blessed
refreshing rain.

Remember

Take from yourself what you will
but don't take from others.
Don't drown yourself in an overload of greed
for you probably already have more than you need.

It's how you're distributing the energy
and sharing out your supply
make sure you have enough fuel to take off and fly.

But remember
nobody said it would be easy
so instead of complaining
find solutions daily
not temporary fixes
tackle problems head on
and completely.

Strawberries & Cream.

I know that we are worlds apart
but there's a force in my mind
entwining the heart.
Left for weeks without the words you provide
but still I feel this something inside.

Trying to drop it off as a phase
you catch me up with your unique ways.

I want to let go
my heart will not profit
wounded but walking
from cupids accidental hit.

Take me back to when I had no clue
of the damage I was about to do.
I'm a deep lover who tends to cling
looking for more than to be a forgetful fling
I don't want to be somebodies play thing.

I seem to be waiting for the dreamed
expectations & possibilities
until I take a quick check on reality
you've shown no signs of wanting me
yet I'm waiting by foolishly.

What can I say
I dared to dream
took a leap into strawberries and cream
came out with just an eating utensil
back to the drawing board with my worn down pencil.
Got to get your attention while your feelings are ripe
haven't you realised by now that i'm willing to try.

It's not just a phase
It's not just hype
I realise it more with each second I live
and with each word that I type.

My mind had already set its focus on you
and now you are all that is in my view.
I just want it to be me connected with you
so I could eventually stumble across those three words …

Imagine Intimacy

Light daring droplets in a fingertips touch
flirting with a fantasy I don't want to give up.
Picturing perfection down to every detail
innocent sensations tingle through without fail.

Your body heat bruises my sensitivity
as your hands explore sexually
romantic sensuality.

Deep breathing silence.
Exhales on the sides of my neck.
Teasing tongue
lips on lips
eyes on the kiss
each time I reminisce
in the moments passing
that passionate kiss.
Body on body
skin presses skin
that shy tension
is now paper thin.

How I'll love it when our warmth is entwined.
Woven in every way
with your legs between mine.

Perched up in the air for our eyes to lock
excitement rushes to the end of my ...
eyebrows
arched in a way
A way to tell you all I can't say.
The next few movements are us being one
thick thighs tangled tightly around my waist

all this magic before we've even begun.

The contrasts in our skin tones
the beauty in our mix
a love so meant to be
beyond what a cherub could fix.

Skin so sexily smooth
just seeing that causes a mind to lose
lose all control in a moment with you.

Take my spirit, mind, body and soul
my heart and love are all yours to own
only because you've lovingly shown
all yours back on the platter.
Your heart and my heart
all those little things that really matter.

I'll love you in a stupendous amount
I wake up hoping for these dreams to sprout.
Imagining intimacy in my dream cloud.

Tension

How far can you go without saying?
How long can you last without spilling?
This story to be told is still laying
on the tip of your tongues release.

When will the truth be spoken?
When will your silence break?
Your heart wasn't made for secrets
and love will conquer in its wake.

Did you know the result of hiding?
Did you guess this books end?
Surely you want what you've dreamt of
and isn't that more than a friend?

Your heart wasn't made for secrets
your eyes gave the plot away
your lips trembled when lying
there was something important to say.

Would you rather not know the answers?
Would you rather sit back and wait?
Hoping the feelings are mutual
pushing yourself out like neglected bait.

You close your eyes to imagine
you shut your mouth tight to stay calm
and now your heart is pounding
as the heat collects in your palms.

Are your signs too blatantly uncovered
that you feel you've already lost?
The fight for that wanted attention
has your presence already been tossed?

The desperation is close on shaking
shivers ricochet down the small of your back
further away your distance is growing
as you doubt all the things that you lack.

Draw closer to that one reason
why you are starting to feel this way
that one person is patiently waiting
to hear what your heart has to say.

Crack open that little secret
that you've so carefully held
love has wings of glory
that darkness must be quelled.

Open your eyes to witness
how close you let yourself get
trust all of your instincts
your heart hasn't failed you yet.

Your heart wasn't made for secrets
your eyes let the barrier fall
they looked inside your stronghold
now unable to stand tall.

Is it too late to retreat?
Do you care what the outcome will be?
You've let them read your pages
and handed over the secrets key.

Will they lock the door behind them
Or will they look for an escape?
Will they caress your heart completely
Or deform your secrets shape?

Your heart wasn't made for secrets
which is why you hurt like you do

let go of that painful burden
and just say it
'I Love You.'

Learning Lasting Love

There's a sweetness in the taste of the drifting heated moment.
Contact with welcomed foreign feelings forced through thriving
curiosity and a warmth of passion pushing past the cold
emptiness of my scent. Silent stillness in the seconds of
bonding amongst the disorder of Neurone City.

I have not yet grasped the liquid fluidity of love in this
intangible capacity. Obtaining that level of understanding I do
not need yet fully acquire, because all I am needing are the light
teasing brushes upon my innocent desire.

It was not designed to be handled in its prematurely fragile
form, only felt like tiny bees with dreams in their stings as they
swarm. I need not collide, crash and collapse into the extent of
its wonders, for I will become nothing but lost as it enchants me
into a deep reverie.

Finding myself not as I currently know myself to be, estranged,
riddled with difficulties in learning how to climb each branch of
the emotion tree. Reaching without the fingers to pull myself
into the next phase of its enlightenment, with all the collected
crawling and evidential experience on the scrapes from knee to
knee.

Falling from this state of illusion will damage hopes seed of the
future promised. Never daring the nearness again out of fear of
losing what I thought I had found. Preparation to meet the
awareness of perfectly perceiving and receiving the feeling. I'll
dip with doubt until i'm out to return after renewing and re-
healing.

Eager to inherit although restless thoughts run rushing,

but occasionally pausing to enjoy, momentarily, involuntarily blushing. That perspiring energy that permits me to plunge into a pool of pleasure. I'm not seeking a temporary thrill for I search only for a love I cannot measure.

I'll wait like the bawling of the wishing wind in the midnight hour. Keeping time on the stars that surface and then gently fade away, resting upon your soundless sleep twitching to your movement as I cower.

Filling myself up with the intentional attempt,
impersonating confidence, to call out your name.
Bringing your ear to the purity that taps on the flicker of a potential flame.

Run away with the trip of visualised atmospheric joys in passions imagination and when light rises with the passing of the morning sun, my vision still blurred between my present reality and the dream of who you are…
two hearts,
our hearts,
could possibly knit so tightly together as one.

The search for you had already begun in a child's fantasy and built-up idealistic inventions.
I've been learning for years how to keep you starting from the laying of our foundations.

Learning of a love that will last.

Tired of Lonely?

Behind the skin deep layers
you hide your precious bounty.
Behind your empty prayers
I see your intentions clearly.

I've caught the wicked repulse
whipped up the side of my back
saw through your mist of lies
watched your stronghold crack.

You threw to me your stories
and you suffocated the truth
to the point of believing it all yourself
both left standing there aloof.

Backing away from danger
fronting up to all my needs
walk past me like a stranger
who knew love could bleed?

You're the constant reminder
that threat to my very being
locked away all emotions
that need desperately freeing.

Drew me close
knocked me down
Sensitive Interior
Who's the clown?
Control and power
all under your thumb
crushed loves hope

until I'm numb.
Why let me in
to shut me out?
Bring me close to whisper
and then intrusively shout
words so unfamiliar
to the plane we were on.
What happened to love
Where has that gone?

Only you could drive me there
this place of nothing
non-existent care.

Pathetic weakness
these unwanted tears
remaining under your spell
and I will do for years.

Getting tired of lonely?

Heart Guardian:

The Love Behind Brown Eyes

Burnt sienna
ambitious amber
drops of hazel dreams.
Rich paradise mixture
that deep swirling texture
of a staring fusion
colour illusion
caught up in this rapture.

Beauty behind perplexity
subtlety in your secrecy.
A crystal ball enigma
secluded stained stigma
pulls me in to know much more.

Velvet auburn
mahogany mystery
taste of chocolate
alluring history
enticing my desire.

Unpublished truth
kept me aloof
drawn back by your appeal.
Spellbound moments
stolen segments
in time being mesmerised.

Cocoa smudge
that final nudge

a pull that magnetised our connection.

The warmth in closeness
as two hands press
taken to the stillness of the skies.
Breath on breath
my heart pounding chest
the love behind brown eyes.

Trust In Time

I'll take you to that place of doubt
just to remind you all the ways out.
Taking you past that danger zone
giving permission to whine and moan.

Pulling it down to level the foot mark
what a phase we're about to embark.

I don't love me so I don't expect love
so when you give love I can't accept love.

Will you survive the passing of me
me diseased with the hatred of me?
Me and every single broken part
decisions are yours, simple or smart.

Hold on tightly
nightly gripping
loving lightly
or deep dipping?

Doubting me because I doubt myself
will you take the escape route out?
I've laid the path for your choosing
Will you withstand the outer bruising?

Cruising through the honeymoon phase
laughter in the ears, an obstacle haze.
I hope you make it
and please don't fake it.

Just love me true to help me understand
take my hand for I can be loved
guide me through to this fantasy land.

Will we make it ?
Let's create it.

I'm learning how.
Trust in time.

Eternity & Forever

My love for you flows deeper than the life keeping me upright
aching for your touch to bring me closer to truth and light.

Your fingertips on my fingertips
sensation on top of sensation.

I'm in control because I want it all
yet so far from it because its very nature is wild
but I don't want it to be tamed.

Hold you closer
so you hear me say your name.
Calling on your pull
to make me feel so full.
Ride together down this rough road.

Eternity and forever.

Spread my hands
through the sheets
to find your heat
to get the key
only you keep.
Body cries
squinted eyes
you make me feel
so complete.

Is it all too much to ask?
Eternity and forever is what you told me
Is that a promise that you can keep?
Because my love for you runs deep.
Deeper than the life that makes my heart pound for you.

I love you
I really do.
Afraid that if I do
My life will be stolen.
What good is a heart that no longer pounds?
Future turned to history
because you don't want to be around.
I'm frightened that you have such power
to rip my world in two
but I love you
I really do.

Drop down from space a feather
never landing love
Eternity and forever.

Deadly Waters

Toss the stone across the water
you think you own the surface.
Net the fish ready for slaughter
you think you own the treasure.

You dove into the doubtful depths
you swam and made your ripple
you struggle to make it back to light
as you watch them start to triple.

You've taken from the floor bed
what was not yours for the taking
t'was not made for your greedy hands
What's this trouble you are making?

You've disturbed the natural flow
you've disrupted the rhythmic drips
now the sun has bounced its glow
air is forced through tight sealed lips.

Are you drowning in your misjudgment?
You thought you could handle the deep
but now you're gasping out for help
holding onto the stolen goods you keep.

I can stare beneath the reflections
but reaching in is an action withheld
a thick wall has grown between us
you won't hear me even if I yelled.

I'll build from faith a floating hope
that you might possibly hold onto
when you've reached the edge of choice
Which one is it you will you rush too?

When you look up to the beams of light
shooting through to your dead journey
pray you survive the pitch black night
when you've drifted far from learning.

You must act fast to change fate now.
You must use your time so carefully.
Only you will know just how
to travel back to heavens pathway.

My heart sinks in my doubting
I pray you see there's so much more
far beyond your way of coping
pick yourself up from the sandy floor
and find your way back to here.

I'll meet you on futures shore.

I Am

I am here
and I am strong
my story is deep
the sentences long.
I am now
not of the past
I grew a feeling
a love that will last.
I am burdened
but never am I weak
I grew fearless
as I climbed to the peak.
What I am not
is not what I am
don't push in lies
clutter and Cram.
I know the truth
silly lies can't clot
I know one thing
what I am not.
And what I am not
is what you want me to be
because I am here now,
strong and free.
I am what I am
and you'll soon see
I know what I am
that will always
be me.

She Flies: The Phoenix

Red haired fire ball
containing bright light
glittering wings that fall
by her side to keep the flight.

Blazing sun rays dazzling vision
frozen clouds stop her in place
blinded into dangerous collision
but saved by Gods good grace.

Passion filled adventure
pounding heart of love
with truth as her teacher
she roams the skies above.

Now she's gliding free from trouble
now resting upon much calmer wind
no need to return to pasts rubble,
to the future her mind is pinned.

You'd think she'd tire from soaring
flying so high for so long
this red haired lioness keeps roaring
secret hidden powers make her strong.

She adapts to the waters
the land, storms and rain.
Not once has she faltered
even under the greatest pain.

Red hair that keeps on burning
like the flame deep in her eyes
wheels of hope and love keep turning
many years of the unthinkable

many years
and still

She flies.

A Message For A Friend.

Laughter lies deep in eyes of life.
Contagious is your radiant light
catching through a smile so bright.
I pray you keep on shining.
Strength holds close in an open heart
flowing love painting a piece of art
a masterpiece of a character you are.
A friend to keep
A spirit so deep
You'll always be
to me
a star.

Fruitless Father

You don't gain respect by raising your fist
you gain respect by raising your kids.

When they grow up to be more than
what you could've dreamt for yourself
A desire to grow, love and learn
not for destruction and polluted wealth.

Can't you see you're poisoning innocent minds
when your tongue lashes lies
like the whip on the back of a slave.
Forced into living by your actions and reactions
Redefining that parenting "behave."
Replacing it all with a lightning fear
you strike and we wait for the sound
mothers screams so we still know she's around.
Still breathing in a bedroom of anger and hurt
crushing her into your box of dusty dirt.
Little did you know who truly controlled our fate
love does not fit into this type of hate.

Love does not make you bleed.
Love does not deny you of what you need.
Love does not take in greed.

Control is not gained through raising your fist
control is gained by raising your kids.
The discipline in love is not a violent thing
it's a process of growth out of mistakes
educating through your parenting.

It is not swinging me around and painting me bruised
choosing to abuse me until I tie my own noose.

Stealing my future by raising your fist.
Loosing my father to those raised fists.

Love is not what you made it to be
that's why those around you
always pick up and flee.
Sadly and unfortunately
it still took a while to be free
because of all that was stolen from me.

Forever fearing father.
Fruitless is the fist that fights the family
but the family fought back with forgiveness.

Exposure to the light brought forth our freedom.

I would love to return to show you one thing
you'll fail to raise your fist to me again
from where i'm standing.

Brief Moments

Brief moments
those that pass me by
from the tip of the tongue
to the corner of my eyes.
That moment I'm alone
with the trembling of my thighs.

Sound begins to muffle
smells stop travelling the air
my feet slowly shuffle
as the wind passes my hair.

My glance has not yet lifted
to the crowd awaiting me
my volume not yet increased
as my heart tries beating free.

I have to catch this moment
grab my heart and keep it there
my feet are now stood frozen
forced to open up and share.

Trickles of words flutter
through the spaces in my mind
I try to gather all in memory
but my sound I cannot find.

I squeeze my eyes shut firm
and the lyrics begin to spring
i'm ready now to give my all
as I open my mouth to sing.

These are such brief moments
those moments that pass me by

from the tip of my tongue
to the corners of my eyes.

Such intimacy and closeness
as I pour out all I can give
the rush of energy is fast
like flour through a sieve.

Such penultimate energy
such power, presence and poise.
Seconds and minutes
absorbing the uplifting noise.

I'm gone.
Now a memory of a feeling
a source of strength
and a therapeutic healing

Now drained empty and waiting
for my brief moment in suspense
with some thing that restores me
and builds back up my defence.

Take Me There

Through thistles and thorns
I walk alone
Through stings of swarms
I am alone.

I will tread along thin wire
until the blood line is seen
dripping on the balance
waiting for the next scene.

Through blindness and dark
I am alone
Through every needle remark
I walk alone.

Company is a thing
only cherished in dreams
a golden glow is expanding
seeping through broken seams.

Lasting it won't be
but treasure it I will
soft to the touch
caught on a thrill.
I'm walking alone
having hours to kill.

Crush the pocket of truth
crack the glass divide
extracting me from here
letting standards slide.

I am alone.
I walk alone.
Searching for that place
A place to call home.

Take me there.

Your Voice

Your Voice
a delicate whisper into a space of silence
a whisper mistaken
for the content of your words were so loud.
Vibrations touching
bouncing from walls
enclosed and hidden
sheltered from misleading teachings.

Your voice
your silent voice
your choice
your silent choice.

The vulnerability in not asking
the beauty in not knowing
always nothing that needs masking
as the sound continues growing.

Without a scratch upon the chord
not a scrape or a jumping second
through this space it surely soared
from a mind to the tip of a tongue.

Your voice
your secret weapon.
The innocence in pure blindness
cut off from their anaesthetisation
living life through endless kindness.

You may think your voice is quiet
but it's loud over conformation

you know your right from wrong
so there's no need for confrontation.

Your tone is triumph
a melody sweet
walking bars of harmony.
Your meaning's deep
the notes they weep
your voice
I pray you keep.

Prance Around The Serious

Tip toe around the subject
prance around the serious
jump into the eye of the storm
avoiding all the mysterious.
Applaud what you have no knowledge of
clap until your palms are sore
you're smiling with doubtful thoughts again
walking sheepishly through life's tour.

Let's get to the seed of the subject
and let us sit in the now serious seat
it may be quiet in the centre of your brain cells
perhaps education and you did not meet.

Let us all focus at what is now unfortunately happening
look at how desensitised and ignorant you've become
a sting in your humour that no longer contains funny
walking lost when you foolishly thought you had won.

So before you go chasing string balls
look at what's pulling the thread
you seem to follow any direction
without even using your head.
You prance around the serious
and now you're the jokers pun
thought you were cool and popular
oh what a web you have spun.

Now trapped inside your own trickery
the world is going to eat you alive
should've opened your mind and listened
you should have had a little more drive.

But now you are regretting the obvious

let's look back at what you have done
every one has the chance to change
lay your foundations before you have fun.

Muddied Waters

Broken down purity
muddied in shallow water
tricked into submission
guardians start to falter.

Ripped apart from familiar
dragged into stacked stale lies
beaten to the nonsensical
not sure whether to live or die.

Surrendering under pressure
persistently pernicious plans
manipulative and destroying
where's the love in these loved hands?

What happened to the promises
that set the golden dream alight?
Where's that same passion
from the beginning of this very fight?

Twisted worm hole magic
disappearing down rabbit holes
slipping self worth still fading
missing all the main route goals.

I can never let go
cut flesh and i'll still hold on
my promise was forever binding
not a trail from crumb to con.

My hearts not easily broken
my mind never greatly swayed
but stolen is my capacity
now I smell myself as I decay.

Gaze on as a witness
like you never played the part
victimless behaviours
as you crush my thumping heart.

Eyes of trust and longing
for change on tomorrows dawn
bloody tear drops unconvincing
as you move me like a pawn.

Promises promises broken
absent in presence by your word
no fight for your blessings
you flee as soon as dangers heard.

The bond that tied the spirits
the pact scratched down in stone
permanent history carved
yet you step like you're not home.

Who is this confused stranger
possessing the sweet sanctuary
parading in such confidence
as if this stench is meant to be?

Cast out the dark heart whisperer
who convinces the most purest of love
to commit the most horrendous crimes
acting as though it fits like a tailored glove.

Memories memories forgotten
of the reasons for creating this
transport to your real life fantasy
perhaps there's something that you missed?

Amongst all the rubbled rubbish
debris of shattered promises

search for the root of entwinement
early prayers and wishes.

To find some one worthy
a match to match the soul
you found the one you wanted
and then you let them them go.

Grab back onto your blessing
before what's yours is stole
hold on to pure love
it's what makes your purpose whole.

Granted there are many tests
that seem to outweigh the good
but blessings don't come easy
so do what you know you should.

Be patient, vigilant and understanding
slow to anger instead be quick to hug.
Above all remember what you have
grab that seed and bury it deep
and don't forget what you have dug.

Love

Love.
A sweet surrender to the senses
a sharp force into your side
tearing down all of your defences
no choice but to run and hide.

Love.
The answer to the end of your sorrows
the beginning of a broken down view
that strength that you need to borrow
the persistent pain that cut you in two.

Love.
An honest hush of innocence
a dark cloud of endless lies
embraced by its presence
cut down by its nasty surprise.

Love.
Joyous overwhelming emotions
pits of depression and despair
so high looking down on foundations
lost without a slash on the bark.
Dreaming of a future together
burnt by a past leaving its mark.

Love.
No one person can describe it in its entirety
love doesn't have a way with words
recollection brings a feeling of self worth
unfamiliar when it is heard.

Do not be convinced love is
what is was defined to you
by that which hurt you
for that was not truly love.

Love is …

Yet to be defined
yet to be truly felt
yet to be described
yet to be had completely.
Love is all over
camouflaged in your doubts
your pain
your guilt
and your lies.

Love is unconditional
never ending
Love.

I Need You Now

I didn't know what was missing
until our lips were kissing
frozen hearts slowly melting
teaching love without doubting
embracing these feelings for you.

A stranger to myself as I dive
asking myself, "Will I survive?"
Holding hands
whilst making plans.

To fall together peacefully
but I can't see how.
I've never known this before
but I need you now.
I'm scared without you by my side
promising wedding vows
I can only hope you need me too
because I need you now.

Dear God

Take my hands and guide me
take my eyes and show me
take my voice and tell me
please, take my life and use me.

Guide me through all the obstacles in life
open my eyes to the many dangers ahead
I have faith that every thing will be alright.
Lord, take my life and show me how to live
live a life full of wonders, lessons and dreams.
Show me how to spread the love you give to me
by teaching me of how to guide others to it
opening their eyes to the dangers in their lives.
Let me use my voice to comfort them
through only words of you.
Above all
Take OUR hearts
and help us make them pure.

Amen.

Zzz...

Unmedicated sleep
my eyes won't keep
from thoughts so deep
keeping me from deep sleep.

Exhausted but not tired
energy pre-consciously hired
my body has been fired
after the days work is done
but my mind's still having fun.

Close my eyes to quiet darkness
and to wondrous colours I start to swoon
as they steal the small spaces
of my eye lids empty drowsy room.
Such limited spots of blankness
spark life into the resting tomb
like the 90's potential
of my mothers waiting womb.

I may as well take its hand to dance
unwillingly yanking my lifeless body like a kite
unknowingly through to the a.m
straight to the early hours of mornings light.

Urm, excuse me Mister eyelids …
what happened to my night?
I just this moment settled my head to sleep
I wasn't prepared for this impromptu fight.

I looked forward to this resting
through the exerting lengthy day
envisioned burrowing into the comfort
luxuries all appreciated as I lay.

I treasure that virgin freshness
of the smooth sea of inviting sheets
but these eyelid presentations
prevent me from snuggling with glorious sleep.

I closed them tightly to fall so deep
and then thoughts so vibrantly loud and sweet
got me lost in being half asleep
but more awake with tapping feet
to the drum of an anti-soporific mesmeric beat.

Slip my vision through the slit of one eye
just to see the blueness of day breaks sky!
What happened to my sleep?
Seize the day they say!
Brave the hours that seem so bright
well, I must beg to differ as
I cosy into my good morning
but Good Night!
Zzz

Break Open

How can I break open my heart
without it all falling apart?
Take out the poison and see
the strength and courage in me.
You've got to break open your heart
so you can set yourself free.

The Thickness Of Our Bark

There are somethings I wish I could un-know
the evil in people that freely continues to grow.
How to lie without batting an eye.
The preconscious judgement we so harshly throw
and how about fear of the deep and unknown.

All learned behaviours implanted into our way of living
taught to be vulnerable and broken to be moulded again
so we continue to take without ever lovingly giving.
Pretending these boys are fully grown men.
Breaking down trust and never forgiving
sorry, my mistake ... did I call this living?

I fear that our people are spiritually cannibalistic
I am scared because you showed me to be afraid
open black hearts are a large grouped statistic
lie to myself to close my eyes to the truth laid
until reality comes and digs in an almighty kick.

I called you out to be bad without realising
that perhaps your struggle went deeper than mine.
the battle with good and evil
took up the life in your precious time.
Consumed all you knew to be light
and locked you out in the dark
we all choose a different fight
different thickness in our bark.

I refuse to fear what I don't know
learn before I judge your whole being
that will focus me on the truth aglow
avoiding the lies that would usually grow
finding that which is freeing.

Evil was fear manifesting
an ill-advised illusion for your inner soul
with that now out of the picture
you're easier to receive as a person whole.

There are some things I wish I could un-know
but that wouldn't be the hurt and the tests
that would remove my characters refining
and the people who add so much flavoursome zest.

You may have bitterness inside you
pain, misery and so much more
but these aren't the things that define you
nor the things given on the day you were born.

There's something i will now remember with priority
something to tell myself when I'm feeling sore
beneath judgement, apparent evil, the lies and the fear
in the beginning it was just purity and love at your core.

Destructive Tears

Destructive are those tears
tears that fall within
tearing apart those layers so thin.
Layers of emotion
delicate like glass
sturdy foundations
all bent like brass

Destructive are those tears
they drop like cannonballs
smashing into your inner walls.
Walls that held up the pain inside
and sealed off hurt you tried to hide.

Destructive are those tears
searched for firm and solid ground
you swam amongst the wreckage
but there was no strength to be found.
Your foundations had been uprooted
your arms had grown tired and weak
how could you lift your head
to a future so uninvitedly bleak?

Dissolving in your own tears
you continued to cry
soaking up all the anguish
like sugar to a fly.

Why do you weep so heavily?
Letting things separate fragmentarily.
Drifting so far you can't reach anymore
not even knowing what you're looking for.

But now the night has passed

and your head has been rested
you open your eyes upon a new day
and you know you're being tested.
You gather yourself to stay afloat
and realise hope has built a boat
you climb on board to see your way
and now that all is clear to see
you were never too far astray.

Your tears blurred your sight
into a future of trials and fight
not to pull and push you down
but to build firm foundations
so you do not drown
in tears of destruction.

Deceiver

It's not always about the lies that you've told
sometimes it's the truth that you have hidden
covering your coal with thin layers of gold
hoping they believe the stories you've written.

Suicidal Possession

Hi,

I am the demon of suicide
you will try to forget me
but i'll never hide
you will pretend that I am gone
but you'll know that you've lied
for I am the demon of suicide.

You'll think you're doing well
until that moment of doubt
that is when i will step in
just when you think i'm out.
I'll comfort and embrace you
with the promise of ending pain
i'll bring up the reasons as to why
build up the case of excuses to die
and when I feel that i'm winning
I will kick you in your side.

Just so you know that no one is there
no one will ever be around enough to care.
Not one persons love will change your mind
I am the only convincing voice you will find.
I will tell you all the things you're wanting to hear
I will sound like innocent truth whispering in your ear.
But when you come to the action of murder
I will no longer need to push you no further
because I'll know that my deluding dutiful job is done
in those last moments you'll know that i've won.

It'll be a choice that you'll conclude and conceive as your own
because i've been here since you were so young.
When daddy was beating mommy and he came in for you
when every marvellous moment shattered
and you had not a clue as to what was required of you.
When people turn away because you're a burden to carry
when true love turns sour and you know you'll never marry.
Instead you turn to me because i've always been near
and i've never let you down in taking away any fear
because you think that death is now the answer
and you can't think of anything better or faster.

To ease a fragmented heart broken in two
parts insidiously and slyly stolen from you.
Remade into an inadequate nothing
now your options seem few:
Continue in your deceptive nightmare?
or step into my promised irrefutable dream?
People will soon get tired of you
because of your broken theme.
You can lean on me and trust my lies
for I am the demon of suicide.

Now you know my falsely innocent intentions
they're as crystal clear as can be
I'll keep you trapped and be all that is deemed to be free.
I've manipulated and twisted all the hallowed things
deliberately clouded your judgement and broken your wings.

The hilarious element for me has always been
you're wrapped around my foul, fatal and fickle finger
you like to think that you're in complete control
until hatred for yourself always comes to linger.
You're an excellent student to my proselytisation
potential to be top of the class
teaching selfless obedient submission
my precognition is that I prompt you to pass.

The one thing I don't want you to know
are those who love you unconditionally
you can do what ever and be what you wish to be
but inside my world you will never see
the future in your powerful life.

I don't want people to ruin my pernicious plans
with their eager encouragement, cordial compliments and
mentality scans.
You don't need friends when you've got persuasive me
I'll force you to convince the others to be distant and flee.

I am the master of malicious manipulation
You can receive blessing after blessing
but no invitation
to witness and truly feel what your worth
never enough for this bountiful earth.

I've only ever gained my forcible power from you
so if you find yourself doing what I wanted from you
just know that i'm being contentedly entertained.
I'll tease you by showing how it was all a trick
but it'll be too late because I take life quick.
I'll have you forever in my dungeon of death
just give me that last and final breath.

Yes, I am the demon of suicide
you'll be curiously reluctant to choose my sinister side
oh, but when you do I'll be a corrupted stubborn stain to
remove
I'll no longer need to make you willingly approve.
You can analyse, scrutinise and try to pick me apart
I'm only here because you allowed me into your heart.
Yes I am the demon of suicide
Will you give me your life?
It has only ever been for you to decide …

2 Corinthians 11:14
"No wonder, for even Satan disguises himself as an angel of light."

Ephesians 6:11
"Put on the full armour of God, so that you will be able to stand firm against the schemes of the devil."

Romans 16:20
"The God of peace will soon crush Satan under your feet. The blessings from our Lord Jesus Christ be upon you."

James 4:7
"Submit yourselves therefore to God. Resist the devil, and he will flee from you."

Ephesians 4:27
"And give no opportunity to the devil."

Matthew 6:13
"And lead us not into temptation,
but deliver us from the evil one."

2 Timothy 2:26
"And that they will come to their senses and escape from the trap of the devil, who has taken them captive to do his will."

Droplets of Change

If there was not but one of many droplets to fall
not but one grain of sand to move
not but at least one to love
what would this world be?

You may think yourself too minuscule to matter
too out of the way to be seen.
Hiding your hands to stay the opposite of what it is to make a
change.
Deliberately painting yourself too much in the dark to step out
into the light.
You can be seen hidden away tucked into your blanket of lies.
Your absence is damaging to the balance
and the damages are growing in numbers.

You may think yourself minuscule
but if it was not for one raindrop to fall, what would grow?
One grain of sand to move upon what would we stand?
If it was not for one person to love!

What would we be?
Where would we be?
Who would we be?

Stand together in the light of positive change
for you are **here** and they can see you!
And the growth of love built on the foundations of ancestors is
sturdy ground upon which we should continue to
grow and love
Love and grow.

Weakening Anger

Anger weakens the insecurities you already possess
by pushing that hate on others you only press
onto your own wounds
and soon there'll be nobody left
to withstand the pain but yourself.

Count Your Blessings

Count your blessings
remember to remember
walking through life
looking for that burning ember.
Glowing in the dark
as a beacon of light
blessings shine brightly
and guide you through the night.

Count your blessings
and try never to forget
people are hidden treasures
treat them like you've first met
With interest and with love
are they in present mind
or the last thing you think of?

Count your blessings
and remember to remember
they won't always be there
from January to December.

So hold those little treasures
let them travel through your veins
blessings are blessings
not chores or restrictive chains.

Remember to remember
to always count your blessings.

Dig A Little Deeper

Demons creeping in through shadowed loneliness
trying to poison your mind in your silences.
Moments freeze in the presence of hidden fear
stealing knowledge to things that made sense.
Wiping a heavy slate clean
love once lived here.

Over thinking churns your stomach past coping.
Long nights
helpless fights inside a being you once knew.
Estranged to yourself as you are now taken over.
Did you know a demon crept in through your weakness?
A darkness that pulled you into unnecessary stress.

All it takes is one push
and it becomes too much to carry.
All it takes is one scratch
and you leak the things you had.
Pushing back
gone off track
visible cracks
start to slack
bring it back
bring it back.

Do you remember how ?
Dig A little deeper.

Identities Lost

Soft white petal
rugged brown terrain
seeds sown deeply
scattering the grain.

Rough dry soil
blooming pollen life
mixture of dirt
husband and wife.

Refused to water
departed responsibilities
sons and daughters
ravaging liabilities.

Launched by mother
to float on winds
to feed her babies
when hope thinned.

Obscured perceptions
distant from viewing
destinations to land
crash without knowing.

Separated from home
where do I belong?
Rugged brown terrain
or by the petals song?

Both rooted anchors
made something new
no one ever told me
how to join the two.

Stuck in the middle
abandoned from either side
they don't understand you
the colouring of your hide.

Left to find the answers
from petal to rough terrain
family are no longer together
the results of fathers strain.

Now a balance uneven
against mother natures wish
some one to cook the dinner
but no one to catch the fish.

Mind lost in confusion
not proud of daddies gun
children expecting fatherhood
instead shot down one by one.
Fell down to soft white petals
cushioning the violent blows
a flowers stem broken
but the damage has not yet shown.

Process disconnected
family no longer mine
no one to reach out to
to question the bloodline.

Limbo of a life
from one thing to the next
searching for identity
becoming more complex.

Growth with soft white petals
foundation in rugged brown terrain
unified and birthed mixed race

and called the boy Jahméne.

So many labels thrown
to push you to the back
they won't be okay with your skin
because they're not okay with white and black.

'Other' is the term they use
to tear you from relating
connecting to both sides
an entitlement from your parents mating.
People aren't sure how to take you
which always ends in hating
you shouldn't lift too high or beat too low
and the shade doesn't need stating.

A concept people find hard to embrace
the features of my face
nothing to do with my spirits grace.
Outcasted from place to place
a history hard to trace
can't build the case.
White and black together laced
is the same as white and black apart
until one race is classed as the human race
you'll never feel the heart.

Until white can be okay with black
and of course vice versa
I will be without a pack

And what is the cost?

Identities Lost.

Dreamers

Night wonders of a life inside a dream
slotting together fragmented pieces
to find out what it all might mean.

Confusion caused from blurry faces
moments lost in flying races
but you're lying in the same place
every night a different dream.

Staring on into a life you aren't able to touch
outcasted in involvement but still able to watch.
When will it all become too much ?
Are you forced to speak the words out loud?

Actions in your day,
repeated from a dream you found
smiles and eyes in the crowd.
Familiar situations.
Realities and dreams.
What does it mean?

What ever you make it
real life or a dream?
My eyes are open,
and now I have seen.

Morning Story

Birds are singing
branches swinging
hear the mornings story.

Leaves fall weak
houses creak
sun will show its glory.

Air tunnels blow
life slowly grows
scattered bits are floating.

Clouds travel in
rain washes sin
no more sugar coating.

Light seeps through
the morning crew
gathers here to start the day.

Let's begin with a smile
for it takes you through
much further on your way.

Suppression

Suppression led to my expression
watched my dreams come to life.

Hand over mouth
hear my mind shout
and pour from other places.

Freedom is where you find it
not under the spell of manipulation and control
but in the dreams I hold.
My prison cold
abusive words told
yet still so much wonder to behold.

Your situation is what you make it
and I make it the song of the morning bird
notes against the rain
the whistle of the winds
drowning all the pain.

Focused on beautiful things
that will last me for a while.

Reality dreaming
flowing with the dancing leaf
no grief
just contagious smiles.

Dream it all out loud.

Roses

I won't give you
wrapped up red roses
however
I'll give you the seeds
to grow them for
forever.

Pretty Path

Right choices have the most
struggles on their path.
Only the devil makes things
look pretty for you
but not in the aftermath.

Intentional Mistakes

Yes
we all make mistakes
but you can't call
a mistake a mistake
blatantly to ones face
if it was part of an intention
in the first place.

Just Ask

I'd rather people ask the questions
than have their assumptions
and make up their own conclusions.

A Memories Ghost

Swift and silent
a reminder of the past
blurred and unfocused
passing us by so fast.

Swirling serenity
crazily confused
they are the moments
that took wings and flew.

Standing in despair
looking longingly lost
murky waters deep
in winters icy frost.
Winds that forever weep
over life willingly tossed.

Ghosts of memories forgotten
ghosts of loving heart songs
ghosts of tortured spirits
all those that once belonged.

Floating in the very centre
and wandering around the edge
either haunting lonely victims
or giving hope with a returning pledge.

Never to leave your side
or to flee this very place
failing to eternally hide
making out their absent face.

Those taken are never missing
those missing are never lost

they still reside in spaces secret
never truly or completely cut off.

Drifting from the coast
forever fading yet never forgotten
the life of a memories ghost.

Salvation

Teaching love to a lust filled heart
extracting truth from wicked lies
assisting in picking the sins apart
you become the oppressor who only tried.

How long before selflessness
becomes self hatred and neglect?
Bitterness and blame
are the only things you now collect.

Burn your attempts in cremation
and leave it all to God
don't entertain the ideas with flirtation
You must leave them to deal
with their own
salvation.

Thorny Temptation

Your eyes were so deceiving
I've fallen under your seductive spell
now I am lost in your wilderness
overgrown pathways lead me to hell.

The thorns dance a wicked dance
the weeds reach out blocking the sun
the ground sucks up my movement
so appealing is the bullet from a gun.

I know that if I stop moving
the night will have its way
creatures will start to ravage
whilst tall trees gently sway.

I stepped with the assumption I was invited
entered this tantalising paradise of promises
but you embezzled all of my given feelings
left here to scratch off the imposters kisses.

Will I make it out alive?
Will I still be all in tact?
Can't shatter the illusions
being fooled by the act.

Your tempting eyes are so deceiving
your very hidden nature so perverse
it seems the only way to make it back
is being driven home within a hearse.

My coffin lowered into the ground
my body lays in apprehensive wait
the roots begin to crush my body
wrapping around me like a snake.

Draining my spirit bone dry
sucking out all of its weight
I realise it was all a spell
but it is all a little too late.
Dragged into your chamber
as you seal my afflicted fate.

Finding Freedom Forgiving Father

Father,

I forgive you.
Not to condone the suffering
but to detach myself from it.

I forgive you.
Not to attach myself in relation
but to distance myself from the connection
for my own protection.

If I bore a child into this world
diamond beauties and rare pearls
innocence and purity
not knowing the surety
of the future ahead.
Grandparents made you
and you were beautiful
a child brought into this world
Is always beautiful.
Innocence and purity.
I forgive you at your core
because beyond the mist
there is surely more
with what parents bore.
A child is always beautiful
and that is at your core.
I forgive you.

Fingers clenched around my neck
as my eyes roll back into my head.
Limp limbs dangling off from the floor
my breath is falling short.

Piercing evil from eyes to eyes
I can't look over in surprise
the look in my fathers eyes
is a daily sight to witness.

No begging or pleading
just bruises and bleeding.
No sympathy or self pity
just a number in a city.
An unfortunate statistic
hidden behind closed doors,
I can't breathe daddy
passing out
beaten to all fours.
I forgive you.

Lifeless body flying
tears no longer crying
just falling from my face
How much can a little boy take?
Until he is unconscious
the brink of in and out
Out and in.
Punches laid into rib cages
one after the other
like flicking pages.
Frail and young
punching me
brown
black
to purple.

I'm numb.
Speechless shame
forgot my name
beaten past refrain
like a grown man
I must've been about nine

but not the only time
my body no longer mine.

Slave to fear
don't make a sound
don't make him hear.
Your presence can't even creep
in case he bursts
and evil seeps.

I forgive you.

Sunny days
washing up chores
scrubbing dirty plates
as hot water pours.
Cutlery and sharp knives
resting at the bottom of the sink
chicken fat and grease
fuming up in a stink.
Speedily rushing through
to succeed at my daily task
a hand grabs the back of my head
I pull over the bravery mask.
A force too great battle with
a strength overpowering mine
my head smashed into the water
embrace myself again because it is time.
I can't hold my breath for forever
as my throats begins to choke
i'm inhaling the water
and my t-shirt's getting soaked.
Just before the in and out
he knees me in my side
wanders off into the garden
as I pull myself together
to try and hide.

I forgive you father.

Screaming rips through my being
the sounds of mother in pain
raping and beating her
we are at this place again.
Shouting out for some one to save her
but no one coming to her aid
he will some day kill her
What deal was the devil paid?

Father, I forgive you.

The many haunting memories that swirl my mind
there are simply too many to list and recall.
It's taken years to pluck up the courage to find
my forgiveness for you,
but Father

I do forgive you.

ABOUT THE AUTHOR

Jahméne, born on the 26th February 1991, is a British Soul/ Gospel/RnB singer and songwriter with a number one debut album under his belt featuring the legendary Stevie Wonder and Nicole Scherzinger. His second album by the same title as this book "Unfathomable Phantasmagoria" showcases his songwriting skills and also features Samuel L. Jackson reading scripture. Jahméne is of Christian faith and also actively campaigns against Domestic Violence with his mother Mandy Thomas, (Artist and Author of "You Can't Run" An autobiographical book.) Jahméne was the first youth ambassador for the charity 'Womens Aid.' He has also fronted and worked along side 'Peace One Day' and 'One For The Boys.' He was nominated for 'Best Newcomer' at the MOBOs and has won an Urban Music Award for 'Best Male Newcomer.' He's the Second place finalist on 2012's Xfactor UK where Nicole Scherzinger was his mentor.

Other Works
as of 2017

Albums

Love Never Fails
Unfathomable Phantasmagoria

Singles

Titanium
Forever Young
Down For Love
Is This The Time?
I Wish
Love

Other Notable Mentions:

You Can't Run By Mandy Thomas.

Social Networks

Twitter:
@Jahmene

Instagram:
@JahmeneOfficial

Facebook:
@JahmeneOfficial

Buy 'Unfathomable Phantasmagoria' Here:
www.smarturl.it/jahmeneUP

25267396R00077

Printed in Great Britain
by Amazon